D1449587

Michal

DID YOU KNOW? PERSIAN JEWS
DISTRIBUTE GREEN ONION DURING THE
SONG "DAYENU AND HIT EACH OTHER WITH
THE STALKS WHEN THE NINTH STANZA
BEGINS.

Seasoned Moments

building community through food

MOMENTS

PASSOVER

Festive Recipes for Spring

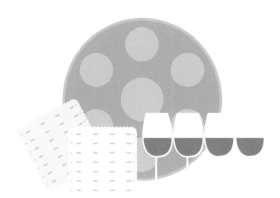

MICHAL LEVISON

Published by Seasoned Moments
www.seasonedmoments.com

ISBN 978-0-9980821-1-0

Designed by Michal Levison
Printed in the USA
First printing, March 2018

TO ZACK, BELLA AND ANYA

CONTENTS

Introduction

My kids LOVE Passover. In this house, Passover is the feast we all look forward to the most. It seems bizarre that a holiday that entails so much work, so much effort and a ton of thought and creativity would be the most cherished! However, the one year we didn't host it, the girls went on and on about their disappointment. We're still hearing about it.

Isn't that funny? Most kids dislike the holiday due to the strict dietary rules associated with it. NO BREAD??? If you look at the holiday from a prohibitionary stance, then it seems confining, even enslaving. Passover celebrates the Israelites' liberation from slavery and passage out of Egypt. Why constrict ourselves in such a way?

Perhaps we should view the rules of Passover as a structure within which we can seek our inner freedom. Seder literally means order. Just as architects build walls in order to create space, we create boundaries in order to savor life. Freedom without limits is anarchy and that is never more obvious than with time, kids or food.

When I have endless time on my hands, I find myself lazy and unproductive. With no deadlines or "must-do" tasks, I just want to lay on the couch and be a sloth. As soon as I put together a schedule (or better yet, take on multiple projects), I find my creative juices flowing and I accomplish so much more. Lucille Ball famously said, "If you want something done, ask a busy person to do it. The more things you do, the more you can do." I guess if you're already juggling several balls, adding one or a few more is not a big deal.

In a similar vein, when my kids have no structure in their lives, they get out of control and whiney. If we give them no boundaries on any given day, I find that they are uncreative and lazy; they whine A LOT and behave poorly. So, we have set up a certain structure and they know our rules. They must practice the piano every day. They help with dinner – whether they cook, set the table or clean up. They must be kind (and there are consequences when they behave poorly that we always follow through on). They know their limits and are free to explore within them, knowing they are safe and secure. Just like in sports, we help them mark the playing field so they know when they're out of bounds. As they grow and we

expand their limits, they will develop confidence and independence that will help them handle responsibility.

When it comes to food – boy is structure needed. Have you ever gone to the grocery store with no plan? Anytime I do that, I end up buying whatever looks good to me and then half of it goes to waste. Why? Because after a long day of work and kids, I don't necessarily feel like competing on an episode of Chopped, figuring out a gourmet meal out of the mishmash of ingredients I brought home. Having a plan (or at least a recipe) helps focus the shopping spree. Before heading to the store, check the pantry, the fridge and the freezer to see there is an ingredient you've been wanting to use but never knew how. Find a recipe using it and supplement with other ingredients at the market. Think of what you want to make in the next two or three days and make a list of missing items. It's even better if you have specific recipes in mind. Make a list and stick to it!

I hope you see this book as the walls that create space for you to flourish. The recipes are merely guidelines – structures within which you should find freedom to explore, and get creative. Spices can be changed. Dressings and sauces can be swapped. Use an idea from one recipe to add new life to another. The kitchen is a wonderful place to assert your freedom. I hope this book helps you find yours for the holiday and all year round. Chag sameach.

Make some magic in your kitchen!

HORS D'OEUVRES

CHOPPED LIVER

INGREDIENTS

6 hard boiled eggs, cooled
1 lb chicken livers, fresh
2 medium onions, chopped
2 garlic cloves, minced
6 tablespoons schmaltz
Salt and pepper to taste

INSTRUCTIONS

In a food processor, pulse the eggs until coarse
chopped. Transfer to a bowl, cover and chill un
needed.

Melt the schmaltz in a medium pan. Sauté onion
and garlic over medium heat until softened, abo
10 minutes.

Meanwhile, pat dry the livers with paper towe
Add them to the pan and increase heat to mediur
high. Sauté, stirring regularly, until the livers a
cooked through, about 8 to 10 minutes. Let cool

Pulse the liver mixture in a food processor un
smooth, then stir into the eggs using a spatu
or wooden spoon. Add salt and pepper to tas
Serve with Tam Tams or other Passover crackers

AVOCADO TZATZIKI

Egg Free

Gluten Free

Nut Free

Serves: 12

INGREDIENTS

avocado
tablespoons yogurt
garlic clove
/4 cup dill
tablespoon lemon juice
/4 - 1/2 teaspoon salt

INSTRUCTIONS

In a food processor, place all the ingredients except the salt. Pulse until smooth.

Season with salt to taste.

Serve with crudite, crackers or a spoon!

BEET DIP
WITH TAHINI AND ZA'ATAR

Egg Free

Gluten Free

Nut Free

Parve

Vegan

Serves: 12

INGREDIENTS

4 medium beets
2 cloves garlic
2 tablespoons tahini paste
3 tablespoons lemon juice
3 tablespoons olive oil
1 tablespoon za'atar
1 tablespoon honey
Salt and pepper to taste

Optional garnishes:
Olive oil
Za'atar
Sliced scallions
Crumbled Feta
Crushed hazelnuts

INSTRUCTIONS

To roast beets: preheat oven to 375°F.

Coat beets with olive oil, wrap in aluminum foil and place on a baking sheet. Roast in the oven for 45 minutes. Let cool, then peel and chop.

Place all the ingredients (except the garnishes) into a food processor and pulse until smooth.

Transfer the dip into a bowl. Drizzle with olive oil and sprinkle with za'atar. Add any other garnishes, then serve with crudité, crackers, or matza.

Note: Galil Achva makes a Kosher for Passover Tahini paste. If you cannot use Tahini, swap 1/2 cup (dairy or non-dairy) yogurt instead the tahini and lemon juice.

EGGPLANT DIP

INGREDIENTS

large eggplant, cut into 1/4 inch rounds
onions, chopped
cloves garlic, minced
tablespoons tahini paste*
live oil
alt and pepper

You can use 1/4 Greek yogurt (or non-airy yogurt) instead

Egg Free

Gluten Free

Nut Free

INSTRUCTIONS

et the oven to high broil.

rizzle eggplant rounds on both sides with oil hen sprinkle with salt and pepper. Place on parchment lined baking sheet. Roast for 7-8 inutes, flipping once, until soft and golden rown. Let cool.

the meantime, sauté onions with two ablespoons of olive oil and a generous pinch f salt over moderate heat. Cook until softened, irring often, then add the garlic. Cook for nother minute then let the mixture cool.

eel away the skin of the eggplant from the ooled rounds. Place eggplants, onion mixture nd tahini (or yogurt) in the bowl of a food rocessor. Pulse until smooth.

Parve

Vegan

Serves: 12

SPINACH STUFFED MUSHROOMS

INGREDIENTS

1 tablespoon olive oil
1/2 onion diced
2 cloves garlic, minced
6 cups spinach
6 cherry tomatoes, chopped
1 tablespoon lemon juice
6 large cremini mushrooms
1/4 cup grated Parmigiano*

*Parve option: omit the cheese

Gluten Free   Nut Free   Parve Option   Vegan   Serves: 8

INSTRUCTIONS

Preheat oven to 375°F. Line a baking sheet with parchment paper.

In a heavy bottomed pan, heat the olive oil over a medium flame. Add the onions and sauté until softened, about 5 minutes. Add in the garlic and cook for a minute while stirring. Add in the spinach and tomatoes and cook until spinach is wilted. Squeeze in the lemon juice and stir to combine.

Meanwhile, stem the mushrooms and brus them with olive oil inside and out.

Stuff the mushrooms and place them the baking sheet. Sprinkle the tops wi cheese.

Bake in the oven for 20 minutes or ur mushrooms have wilted and cheese h melted.

SPICED LAMB MEATBALLS

INGREDIENTS

For the meatballs:
2 lbs ground lamb
1/2 cup fresh parsley, minced
1/2 cup fresh dill, minced
5 cloves garlic, minced
2 tablespoons paprika
1 tablespoon ground cumin
1/2 teaspoon ground coriander
1 1/2 teaspoons salt
1 teaspoon black pepper
1/2 teaspoon cayenne pepper

For the sauce:
1 onion, chopped
5 cloves garlic, minced
28 ounce can crushed tomatoes
1/2 cup fresh parsley, chopped
1/2 cup cilantro, chopped
2 tablespoons pomegranate molasses
1 tablespoon fresh lemon juice
1 teaspoon salt
1/2 teaspoon black pepper
1/4 cup water

 Egg Free
 Gluten Free
 Nut Free
 Serves: 8

INSTRUCTIONS

Line a baking sheet with foil.

Make the meatballs: mix all the meatball ingredients in a bowl. Form into 1" meatballs and place on the baking sheet.

Add 2 tablespoons to a heavy bottomed skillet and heat over a medium high flame. Sauté half the meatballs, flipping regularly, until browned on all sides. Transfer to a plate and sauté the remaining meatballs.

Make the sauce: add a tablespoon of oil to the empty skillet. Sauté the onions until softened, about 4 minutes. Add the garlic and cook for another minute. Add in the remaining ingredients and stir to combine.

Add in the meatballs and stir to cover them in sauce. Cook for another 15-20 minutes. To test meatballs for doneness, cut one in half.

FOR THE SEDER

WHITE MAROR

INGREDIENTS

1 horseradish root, peeled
1 teaspoon salt
1/4 cup white vinegar

INSTRUCTIONS

Cut the horseradish root into one inch chunks and place into the bowl of a food processor. Add the salt and pulse until finely shredded.

Let the horseradish sit in the food processor for 4 minutes to produce heat.* Add the vinegar and pulse to blend.

If it's too spicy, add water, one tablespoon at a time until you reach the desired level of heat.

Be careful when you transfer the horseradisn to a jar - the fumes are intense! Store in the refrigerator. In an airtight container, the horseradish can last up to 3 weeks, but it may lose some heat over time.

Egg Free
Gluten Free
Nut Free
Parve
Vegan
Serves: 12

INGREDIENTS

1 horseradish root, peeled
1 teaspoon salt
1 beet, roasted and peeled
1/4 cup white vinegar

RED MAROR

INSTRUCTIONS

Follow the directions for the white maror.

*Add the beet when you add the vinegar the shredded horseradish. This one will not b as spicy as the white maror, but still take ca when transferring from the food processor your airtight jar.

KARPAS

INGREDIENTS

1 bunch parsley
Enough potatoes for your group

INSTRUCTIONS

I like to serve both parsley and fingerling potatoes for my Karpas.

For the parsley, simply place the branches in a bowl and serve with a salt water dipping bowl alongside.

For the potatoes, boil as many fingerlings as you have attendees in a pot of water until they are fork tender. Place the potatoes in a bowl with salted water.

---

minutes.

Transfer the eggs into a bowl of cold water. After two minutes, gently crack the shell, exposing a little bit of egg and place back into the water. The water will get into the egg and push away at the shell.

After a minute in the bowl, the egg will easily peel into a perfect little orb.

Make ahead - boil and peel the eggs the day before. Store them in water in the fridge.

BEITZAH

INGREDIENTS

As many eggs as needed
Water

INSTRUCTIONS

Boil water in a pot (enough to cover eggs) over medium high heat. Add eggs into the water with a slotted spoon. Turn the heat down to medium low and cook for ten

SIMPLE CHAROSET

Egg Free

Gluten Free

Parve

Serves: 12

INGREDIENTS
2 Honeycrisp apples, cored and peeled
2 Granny Smith apples, cored and peeled
1 cup walnuts, chopped
1/2 cup sweet red wine (Malaga or Concord)
1 1/2 teaspoons ground cinnamon
1 tablespoon honey

INSTRUCTIONS
Chop the apples into 1/4 inch cubes then place in a bowl. Add the walnuts and stir together. Add the wine, cinnamon and honey and mix well. Cover and refrigerate until ready to use.

TROPICAL CHAROSET

INGREDIENTS
1 mango
1/2 pineapple
1/2 cup pomegranate seeds
1/4 cup shredded coconut
1/2 cup sliced almonds
1 teaspoon fresh ginger, grated
1 tablespoon lime juice
1 teaspoon honey
1/2 cup sweet white wine

MIDDLE EASTERN CHAROSET

INGREDIENTS

- cup dried figs
- cup dried apricots
- 1/2 cup raisins
- cup roasted hazelnuts
- blood oranges
- 1/4 cup honey
- tablespoons pomegranate molasses
- teaspoon cinnamon
- 1/4 teaspoon allspice
- 1/4 teaspoon nutmeg
- 1/4 cup orange juice

INSTRUCTIONS

Place all the ingredients in the bowl of a food processor. Pulse until smooth (unless you prefer a bit chunky).

Egg Free

Gluten Free

Parve

Serves: 12

INSTRUCTIONS

Chop mango and pineapple into 1/4 inch cubes. Place all the ingredients in a bowl and mix together until combined. Refrigerate until ready to use.

STARTERS

INGREDIENTS

For the fish stock:
Heads, bones and skin of two fish
4 quarts water
1 tablespoon salt
1 teaspoon sugar
1 large onion, sliced
3 carrots, peeled

For the Gefilte Fish:
10-12 cups fish stock
1 carrot
1 medium onion
1 celery stalk
3 cloves garlic
1/4 cup dill
1/4 cup parsley
1 tablespoon scallions
2-3 lbs cod fillet
2 teaspoons salt
1 teaspoon black pepper
3 eggs
1 tablespoon olive oil
6 tablespoons matza meal

Nut Free

Parve

Yield: 24

INSTRUCTIONS

For the fish stock:
Place all the ingredients in a large, wide pot and bring to a boil. Cover and simmer for 20 minutes (prepare the fish mixture in the meantime).

If you prefer, you can use water, vegetable or chicken stock instead of making a fish stock. Just heat the liquid in a large, wide pot before you make your fish.

GEFILTE FISH

For the gefilte fish:
Place the carrot, onion, celery, garlic, dill, parsley, scallions and chili pepper (if using) into the bowl of a food processor. Pulse until everything is finely chopped. Add the fish, salt and pepper and pulse until the fish is well ground but not liquefied or pasty.

Transfer the fish mixture into a large bowl. Add the egg, oil and matza meal into the bowl and mix until combined.

Wet your hands with water before making each gefilte patty. Round the mixture with your hand and form into an oval shape. Form all the patties and place them on a platter. Add the patties in batches to the simmering stock and cook for 20 minutes, flipping them halfway through.

Using a slotted spoon, gently lift them out of the pot and let them cool on a plate. If you are serving immediately, plate them with a slice of carrot and a sprig of dill and/or parsley on top.

If you are making the fish ahead of time, place them in a baking dish, cover them with the poaching liquid and refrigerate over night. To freeze, place patties on a parchment lined sheet pan. Freeze them in a single layer (for an hour or two) then place them all in a freezer bag. Freeze the poaching liquid separately. To reheat, bring poaching liquid to a boil then simmer the patties for a minute on each side.

CHICKEN SOUP

Egg Free

Gluten Free

Nut Free

Serves: 12

INGREDIENTS

1 parsnip
1 turnip
1 celery root
3 large carrots, peeled
2 onions
4 cloves garlic
1 whole chicken
5 whole legs
Water
1 tablespoon salt
1 teaspoon black pepper
4 celery stalks
1 bunch parsley
1 bunch dill

INSTRUCTIONS

Cut vegetables in half.

In a 12 quart pot, place all the ingredients except celery, parsley and dill. Cover with wate leaving an inch from the top. Gently place celery, parsley and dill and close the lid.

Cook the soup for at least an hour and up to four hours (start tasting it after an hour until yo reach your desired flavor). Strain the soup and pull the chicken.

GARLIC AND DILL MATZA BALLS

INGREDIENTS

[large eggs
3 cup schmaltz
1/4 teaspoons salt
tablespoon baking powder
4 teaspoon pepper
tablespoon parsley, finely chopped
tablespoons dill, finely chopped
tablespoon garlic powder
1/3 cup matza meal

INSTRUCTIONS

Fill a large, wide pot 2/3 full with water, add a generous pinch of salt and bring to a boil.

In the meantime, crack the eggs into a large bowl and beat thoroughly with a whisk until frothy. Beat in the schmaltz, salt, baking powder, pepper, parsley, dill and garlic powder. Switch to a spatula and mix in the matza meal until completely blended.

Wet your hands and shape the dough into balls, about an inch in diameter - the balls will double in size when cooked.Gently place the matza balls in the boiling water and reduce heat to low.

Cook for 25 minutes, then remove with a slotted spoon.

Make ahead: you can cook the matza balls, remove from the pot and place them on a cookie sheet lined with parchment. Freeze until solid then transfer to a freezer bag. To reheat, simply simmer in hot soup for 20-30 minutes.

Nut Free

Yield: 14

Making matza balls has become an obsession for my girls. One year, they came down and said, "Put us to work like Avadim Hayinu (slaves in Egypt)!" They make around 100 "Monster Balls" for our Passover Seder.

CARROT SOUP
WITH PARSLEY GREMOLATA

INGREDIENTS

For the gremolata:
Peel of a whole lemon
1 cup parsley
4 cloves garlic
3 tablespoons olive oil

For the soup:
2 tablespoons olive oil
1 large onion, chopped
2 lbs carrots, peeled and sliced
5 cups vegetable stock or water
3 garlic cloves, peeled
1 1/2 teaspoons cumin
1 1/2 teaspoons paprika
1 1/2 teaspoons salt
1 teaspoon honey
1/2 teaspoon ground black pepper

Egg Free

Gluten Free

Nut Free

Parve

Vegan

Serves: 12

INSTRUCTIONS

Prepare the gremolata: place all the ingredients in the bowl of a food processor. Pulse until blended. If it needs thinning, add more oil just a little at a time.

Make the soup: In a soup pot over a moderate flame, heat up the olive oil. Sauté the onion and carrots until softened, about five minutes.

Add the remaining ingredients and bring to a boil. Lower the heat and simmer until the carrots are fork tender, about 20 minutes.

Cool slightly then puree in a blender (or use an immersion blender in the pot).

Serve with a swirl of the gremolata.

ASPARAGUS SOUP

Egg Free

Gluten Free

Nut Free

Parve

Vegan

Serves: 12

INSTRUCTIONS

Preheat oven to 425°F.

Cut the tips from the asparagus and set aside. Cut the remaining spears into 1" segments.

In a heavy bottomed pot, cook the onion in the olive oil over moderate heat, stirring often until softened, about 6-7 minutes.

Add the stock, asparagus segments (not the tips!), zest, lemon juice and salt. Simmer the soup until the asparagus is tender, about 30 minutes.

While soup simmers, roast the tips: toss them in a tablespoon of olive oil and 1 teaspoon of salt. Place them in one layer on a parchment lined baking sheet and roast

INGREDIENTS

2 lbs asparagus, trimmed
2 tablespoons olive oil
1 large onion, sliced
5 cups chicken or vegetable stock
Zest of half a lemon
1 tablespoon lemon juice
1/2 teaspoon of salt

in the oven for 7-8 minutes or until lightly charred.

Purée soup in batches in a blender until smooth, transferring to a bowl (use caution when blending hot liquids). Season with salt and pepper.

Garnish with asparagus tips.

BITTER HERBS
WITH A DIJON VINAIGRETTE

INGREDIENTS

For the salad:
1 head Romaine lettuce
1 head radicchio
2 heads Belgian endive
2 cups arugula
2 scallions
1/4 cup parsley, chopped
1/4 cup dill, chopped
1/4 cup mint, chopped

For the dressing:
1/4 cup sherry vinegar
1 teaspoon Dijon mustard
1 shallot, minced
1 teaspoon honey*
1/2 cup olive oil
1/4 teaspoon salt
1/8 teaspoon pepper

Egg Free

Gluten Free

Nut Free

Parve

Vegan Option

Serves: 12

INSTRUCTIONS

Slice the various lettuce heads and place in a bowl with the chopped herbs.

Make the dressing: in a small bowl, whisk together all the ingredients until blended well. Tas
and adjust the seasoning by adding salt and pepper, if necessary.

Drizzle the dressing and gently toss the salad to make sure everything is coated.

*Vegan option: replace honey with maple syrup

BERRY SALAD
WITH BEETS AND ALMONDS

INGREDIENTS

or the salad:

b mesclun or spring green mix
cup beets, chopped into cubes
2 cup blackberries
2 cup pomegranate seeds
2 cup scallions, chopped
3 cup roasted almonds, chopped
ounces Parmigiano, shaved*

or the dressing:

tablespoons lemon juice
clove garlic, minced
2 teaspoon sea salt
tablespoons honey**
4 cup extra virgin olive oil
reshly ground black pepper
3 cup parsley, finely chopped

Parve option: omit the cheese

*Vegan option: replace honey with
aple syrup and omit the cheese

INSTRUCTIONS

o make the dressing, combine the
emon juice, garlic, salt, honey, olive oil
nd black pepper in a bowl. Whisk until
mooth. Gently, blend in the parsley.

lace the salad greens, beets, blackberries,
om seeds, scallions, and almonds in a
rge bowl. Pour in the dressing, and toss
ntil combined. Season with salt and
epper if needed. Shave the Parmigiano
n top and toss gently to combine.

Egg Free

Gluten Free

Parve Option

Vegan Option

Serves: 8-10

SPINACH SALAD
WITH FIGS AND PECANS

Egg Free

Gluten Free

Parve

Vegan

Serves: 8-10

INGREDIENTS

2 tablespoons olive oil
1 medium red onion, sliced
10-12 dried figs, chopped
2 tablespoons brown sugar
2 tablespoons sherry wine vinegar
1/2 teaspoon salt
10 ounces baby spinach
1/2 cup toasted pecans, chopped

INSTRUCTIONS

In a medium pan, sauté the onions the olive oil over moderate heat un softened (about 4-5 minutes).

Stir in the figs, brown sugar, wine vineg and salt and simmer until the figs are fu coated.

In a large bowl, combine the spinac pecans and fig mixture. Toss to coat.

ASPARAGUS
WITH RADISH AND MINT

INGREDIENTS

For the salad:
1 lb asparagus
2 Persian cucumbers
5 radishes, sliced
1 cup cherry tomatoes, cut in half

For the dressing:
1/4 cup lemon juice
1/3 cup olive oil
1/2 teaspoon dried or fresh oregano
2 teaspoons honey*
2 teaspoons Dijon mustard
1 tablespoon fresh mint, chopped
Salt and pepper to taste

*Vegan option: replace honey with maple syrup

Egg Free	Gluten Free	Nut Free
Parve	Vegan Option	Serves: 8-10

INSTRUCTIONS

Using a vegetable peeler, slice the asparagus and cucumber into thin strips.

Make the dressing: in a small bowl whisk together the ingredients until lightly emulsified. Taste and adjust the seasoning by adding salt and pepper, if necessary.

Gently toss all the vegetables together with the dressing and turn out onto a platter.

MAIN DISHES

CHAROSET BRAISED CHICKEN

INGREDIENTS

8 whole chicken legs
3 large onions, sliced
2 carrots, chopped
2 cups charoset
3 cups chicken stock

Egg Free

Gluten Free

Serves: 8

INSTRUCTIONS

Preheat the oven to 350°F.

In a large Dutch oven over a medium-high flame, heat 2 tablespoons of oil. Add the chicken to the pot in one layer and cook until browned, 5 minutes per side. Remove the chicken to a platter and repeat with remaining legs, adding more oil if the pot seems dry.

Add onion, carrot, charoset and a teaspoon of salt and cook, stirring occasionally, until the vegetables have softened nicely, approximately 10 minutes.

Return all the chicken to the pan, skin side up. Add between 1 and 3 cups of chicken stock, enough to come up the sides of the chicken but not to submerge them. Bring to a simmer, cover and then put the pot the oven.

Cook until the chicken is very tender, between 45 minutes to an hour.

BEEF SHANKS
BRAISED IN RED WINE

INGREDIENTS

10-12 ounces beef shanks
salt
freshly ground black pepper
2 tablespoons olive oil plus 2 more
2 carrots, peeled and diced
2 celery ribs, diced
1 yellow onion, diced
4 garlic cloves, sliced
2 cups red wine
2 cups chicken stock
2 cups crushed tomatoes
4 sprigs fresh thyme
1 sprig fresh rosemary
1 bay leaf

Garnish:
1 tablespoon horseradish
2 tablespoons lemon zest, grated
2 tablespoons fresh parsley, chopped

Egg Free

Gluten Free

Nut Free

Serves: 6

INSTRUCTIONS

Preheat oven to 325°F.

Season the shanks on both sides with salt and pepper.

In the bottom of a large Dutch oven (I love my 9 quart Le Creuset), sear the beef shanks in the olive oil over medium high heat until browned, about 4-5 minutes per side. Do in batches, if necessary. Transfer to a plate.

Add another two tablespoons of olive oil to the pan.

Sauté the carrots, celery, onion and garlic for two minutes, until softened. Pour in the wine and cook until reduced by half. Add the remaining ingredients and bring to a boil. Add the shanks back to the pan, close the lid and cook in the oven for 2 1/2 - 3 hours.

Remove the herbs from the sauce. Plate the shanks with horseradish, zest and parsley on top. Ladle vegetables and sauce around the beef.

PRIME RIB
WITH HORSERADISH CHIMICHURRI

INGREDIENTS

For the prime rib:
5-10 lb prime rib
1-2 tablespoons salt
2 teaspoons black pepper
1 1/2 tablespoon garlic powder
1 1/2 tablespoon onion powder
1 head of garlic, top cut off

For the chimichurri:
1/4 cup red wine vinegar
2 teaspoon salt
4 cloves garlic
1 1/2 cup fresh cilantro, chopped
1 1/2 cup fresh parsley, chopped
3 tablespoons horseradish
1/2 teaspoon black pepper
3/4 cup olive oil

Egg Free

Gluten Free

Nut Free

Serves: 6-10

This will knock the socks off your guests! On its own, the meat is delicious and salty. With the chimichurri, it is bright and zingy! If you can, do the final 500 degree roast half an hour before serving the prime rib.

INSTRUCTIONS

The night before you cook it, place the prime rib in a roasting pan. Cover it in salt (you can over salt the meat!) and place in the fridge (uncovered) overnight. This will dry the exterior and create a beautiful crust.

Make the chimichurri: place all the ingredients except the olive oil in the bowl of a food processor and pulse until well mixed. Transfer to a bowl and mix in the olive oil. Cover and refrigerate until needed.

In the morning, cover the rib roast with foil or cling wrap and bring to room temperature (about an hour). Preheat the oven to 225°F. Mix the black pepper, garlic powder and onion powder and spread evenly all over the meat.

Drizzle olive oil all over the head of garlic.

Place the garlic and the rib roast (fat side up) in a roasting pan. Roast in the oven until center of the roast reads 120°F on a meat thermometer, about 4-5 hours.

Remove the prime rib from the oven and cover with foil. Let the meat rest for 30 minutes and up to an hour.

Heat the oven to 500°F and roast the prime rib, uncovered, for 6-10 minutes or until crisp and browned. For medium rare, the thermometer should read 135°F.

Remove from the oven. Let the meat rest for 10 minutes. Carve and serve with chimichurri.

SHAWARMA SPICED LEG OF LAMB

INGREDIENTS

1/2 cup olive oil
1 head of garlic, minced plus 3 cloves, sliced
2 tablespoon cumin
1 1/2 teaspoon ground coriander
1/2 teaspoon cayenne pepper
2 teaspoons smoky paprika
1 1/2 teaspoons turmeric
1/4 teaspoon cardamom
1/4 teaspoon cloves
1 tablespoon salt
1 1/2 teaspoons ground black pepper
1 (8 lb) leg of lamb

Egg Free   Gluten Free   Nut Free   Serves: 8-10

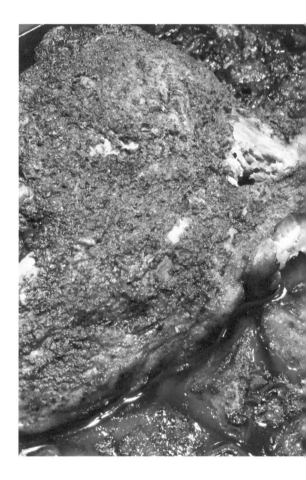

INSTRUCTIONS

Preheat the oven to 350°F.

In a bowl, combine all the ingredients (except the lamb and sliced garlic). Stir to make a paste.

Place lamb into a roasting pan and cut small slits on both sides of the leg. Insert a slice of garlic into each slit. Cover the lamb completely with the paste.

Roast the lamb in the oven for 2 1/2 hours or until a meat thermometer inserted in the thickest part of the meat registers 130 degrees.

Transfer to a cutting board and let stand to 25 minutes before slicing.

Add wine to pan and deglaze by boiling over medium heat, stirring and scraping up brown bits, about a minute. Season pan juices with salt and pepper and serve with the lamb.

RED SNAPPER
EN PAPILLOTE

INGREDIENTS

Per portion:
red snapper fillet
1/2 teaspoon olive oil
teaspoon Mirin or sweet white wine
1/4 teaspoon salt
1/8 teaspoon black pepper
1/8 teaspoon onion powder
1/8 teaspoon garlic powder
slices lemon
sprigs parsley

Parchment paper

Note: Make as many portions as needed

Egg Free

Gluten Free

Nut Free

Parve

Yield: 1

INSTRUCTIONS

Preheat oven to 425°F.

Cut a 12" piece of parchment paper and lay it on a baking sheet. Place your fillet in the middle. Drizzle the olive oil and wine, then sprinkle the salt, pepper, garlic powder and onion powder to cover the fish. Lay the lemon slices and parsley on top, then fold the paper like an envelope to enclose the fish, making sure the flap is on the underside so the envelope won't open in the oven.

Bake for 12-15 minutes, or until fish is opaque throughout. Serve with a sprinkle of parsley and a slice of lemon.

My children are obsessed with "paper fish." It's super simple to make but has a ton of flavor.

ALMOND PISTOU CRUSTED COD

Egg Free

Gluten Free

Parve

Serves: 6

INGREDIENTS

4 cups fresh basil
1 cup fresh parsley
1/3 cup almonds
1/4 cup cherry tomatoes
3 cloves garlic
1/2 cup olive oil
Optional: 2/3 cup Parmesan, grated

6 portions of cod (1"x4")

6 slices of lemon

INSTRUCTIONS

Preheat oven to 425°F.

Make the pistou: place the basil, parsley, almond, tomatoes and garlic and Parmesan (if using) in the bowl of a food processor. Pulse until finely grated. Slowly, drizzle in the olive oil just until a paste forms.

Place the fish on a parchment lined baking sheet about 1-2 inches apart. Cover the tops of the fish (like frosting) with the pistou. Lay a lemon slice on each piece.

Bake for 13-15 minutes or until fish is opaque throughout.

ROASTED SALMON
WITH ASPARAGUS AND LEMON

Meat

Meat

Meat

Meat

INGREDIENTS

2 cup olive oil
bunches asparagus, ends trimmed
tablespoons garlic, minced
3 cup freshly squeezed lemon juice
teaspoon salt
2 teaspoon black pepper
(5 ounce) salmon fillets
tablespoons fresh parsley, chopped
tablespoons dill, chopped

emon, sliced (for garnish)

INSTRUCTIONS

Preheat oven to 425°F. Line a baking pan with foil.

Rub salmon all over with 1 teaspoon oil, place (skin-side down) on the baking sheet and season with salt and pepper.

Toss asparagus with garlic, lemon juice, salt and pepper. Arrange asparagus around the salmon on the baking sheet.

Roast until fish is just cooked through, about 12 minutes. Lift flesh from skin with a metal spatula and transfer to a plate. Discard skin, then drizzle salmon with oil and sprinkle with herbs. Serve with asparagus and fresh slice of lemon.

SIDE DISHES

HASSELBACK PURPLE POTATOES

INGREDIENTS

6 purple potatoes
4 tablespoons olive oil
3 cloves garlic, minced
3 tablespoons parsley, chopped
1 teaspoon salt
6 tablespoons butter (or schmaltz)*

*Vegan or parve option: omit butter/
schmaltz and use a bit of olive oil if
potatoes look too dry

INSTRUCTIONS

Preheat oven to 425.

Place a potato between two chopsticks for
stability and knife guidance. Every 1/4 inch,
slice until the knife hits the chopsticks. (The
chopsticks will help prevent the knife from
cutting all the way through the sweet potato.)
Repeat with the remaining potatoes.

Place the potatoes on a parchment lined baking
sheet. In a bowl, mix together the olive oil, garlic,
parsley and salt. Brush the potatoes with olive
oil mixture, making sure to get in between the
crevices. Top each potato with a tablespoon of
butter (or schmaltz).

Bake for 40 minutes or until soft.

Egg Free | Gluten Free | Nut Free

Parve Option | Vegan Option | Serves: 6

SWEET POTATO
WITH POMEGRANATE AND DATES

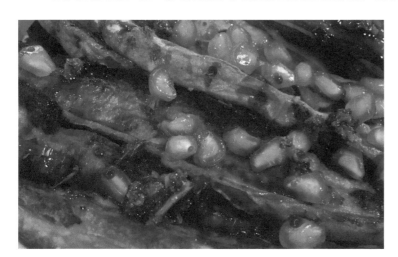

Parve Option

Egg Free

Vegan Option

Gluten Free

Serves: 6

Nut Free

INGREDIENTS

sweet potatoes
¼ cup olive oil plus 1 tablespoon
teaspoons salt
teaspoon black pepper
tablespoons balsamic vinegar
tablespoon date syrup
jalapeño, cut in half
2 dates, chopped
cup pomegranate seeds
tablespoons parsley, chopped

INSTRUCTIONS

Preheat oven to 450°F.

Cut each sweet potato in half and each half into three long wedges. Toss with olive oil, salt and pepper then spread them, skin side down, on a parchment lined baking sheet. Roast in the oven for 20-25 minutes.

In a pan over medium heat, bring balsamic vinegar, date syrup and jalapeño to a boil, then lower the flame and simmer for 4 minutes, until reduced by nearly half. Discard the jalapeño and add 1 tablespoon of olive oil

Place sweet potatoes on a serving dish. Scatter dates and pomegranate seeds all over. Drizzle the vinegar reduction all over and sprinkle with parsley.

SCHMALTZ SMASHED POTATO

INGREDIENTS

8 Yukon Gold potatoes
1/3 cup olive oil
3 cloves garlic, minced
2 teaspoons salt
1 tablespoon schmaltz
2 sprigs rosemary

1-2 tablespoons fresh parsley for garnish

INSTRUCTIONS

Preheat the oven to 450°F.

Add potatoes to a large pot and fill wi
water until the potatoes are just covere
Bring to a boil over medium-high heat, the
cook uncovered for another 15-20 minute
or until potatoes are fork tender.

Meanwhile, mix the olive oil, garlic, salt ar
schmaltz in a bowl.

Drain the potatoes and place them o
a parchment lined cookie sheet. Using
cup or jar, smash the potatoes. Drizzle th
potatoes with olive oil mixture and plac
rosemary sprigs on top.

Roast for 20-25 minutes or until golde
brown and crisp. Garnish with fresh parsle

Egg Free

Gluten Free

Nut Free

Serves: 8

SHISHITO PEPPERS

WITH LEMON AND CHEDDAR

Egg Free

Gluten Free

Nut Free

Serves: 6

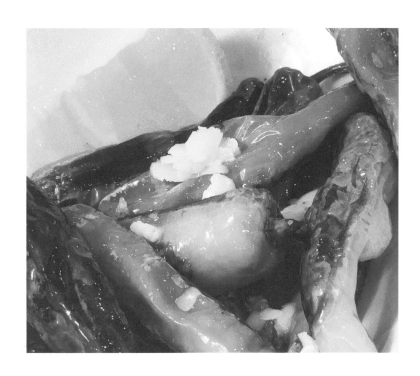

NGREDIENTS

tablespoon olive oil
 ounces shishito peppers
teaspoon salt
alf of a lemon
/4 aged cheddar, shredded

INSTRUCTIONS

Heat the olive oil in a large pan over medium-high heat. Cook the peppers, turning frequently, until they char just a bit and blister on all sides.

Transfer peppers to your serving dish and sprinkle with salt. Squeeze lemon juice on top and toss with shredded cheddar.

MODERN TSIMMES

INGREDIENTS

2 teaspoons orange zest, grated
2 tablespoons fresh orange juice
1/4 cup maple syrup
3 tablespoons olive oil
1/2 teaspoon ground cinnamon
2 teaspoons salt
2 lb carrots, peeled
2 large onions, sliced

Egg Free

Gluten Free

Nut Free

Parve

Vegan Option

Serves: 8-10

INSTRUCTIONS

Preheat the oven to 375°F.

In a bowl, mix the orange zest, juice, maple syrup, olive oil, cinnamon and salt. Toss the carrots and onions to coat.

Spread the carrots and onions on a foil or parchment lined baking sheet.

Roast for 20 minutes or until brown and very tender.

OVEN ROASTED TOMATOES

Egg Free

Parve

Gluten Free

Vegan

Nut Free

Serves: 10

INGREDIENTS

tomatoes, sliced into 1/2" thick rounds
tablespoons olive oil
cloves garlic, minced
sprigs thyme, chopped finely
1/2 teaspoons salt
2 teaspoon ground pepper

INSTRUCTIONS

Preheat the oven to 375°F. Line a baking sheet with parchment paper.

In a bowl, mix the olive oil, garlic, thyme, salt and pepper.

Lay the tomato slices in a single layer on the baking sheet. Brush the top of the tomatoes with the olive oil mixture. Drizzle any remaining oil on top of the tomatoes.

Bake for 30-40 minutes or until tomatoes start to brown.

SWISS CHARD
WITH LEEKS

Egg Free

Gluten Free

Nut Free

Parve

Vegan

Serves: 6-8

INGREDIENTS

1 bunch Swiss chard
1 bunch leeks
Olive oil
Salt and pepper

INSTRUCTIONS

Preheat the oven to 350°F. Line a baking sheet wi
parchment paper.

Cut the stems out of the Swiss chard, then slice th
leafy parts into thin ribbons.

Slice the leeks into thin rounds.

Spread the Swiss chard and leeks on the bakir
sheet. Drizzle with about 3 tablespoons of olive c
You may need more to coat them through, Sprink
with salt and pepper and toss everything to coat.

Bake for 15 minutes but watch them carefully. The
quickly go from perfectly soft to burnt.

CACIO E PEPE ASPARAGUS

INGREDIENTS

1 lb asparagus
2 tablespoons olive oil
1/2 teaspoon black pepper
1/4 teaspoon salt
1/3 cup of Parmesan, grated
1 tablespoon lemon juice

Egg Free

Gluten Free

Nut Free

Serves: 8-10

INSTRUCTIONS

Preheat the oven to 375°F. Line a baking sheet with parchment paper.

Break off or trim the bottom of the asparagus.

In a large bowl toss asparagus, olive oil, black pepper, salt, 1/4 cup of Parmesan and the lemon juice until well coated.

Lay asparagus in a single layer on baking sheet and bake for 10 minutes or until lightly browned. Let rest for 5 minutes.

Top with the remaining Parmesan and a few more cranks for fresh ground black pepper before serving.

ROASTED ARTICHOKES

INGREDIENTS

3 artichokes
6 large cloves garlic
1 lemon plus 6 slices
Olive oil
Salt
Black pepper

Egg Free • Gluten Free • Nut Free
Parve • Vegan • Serves: 6-8

INSTRUCTIONS

Preheat oven to 400°F. Line a cookie sheet with parchment paper.

Cut 1" from the top of each artichoke and trim the stems. Cut each artichoke in half and rub the cut side with lemon (or it will brown).

Scoop the fuzzy choke from the middle of each artichoke half and rub olive oil all over. Place a garlic clove in the center of each artichoke and cover with a slice of lemon.

Place the artichoke lemon/cut side down on the cookie sheet and drizzle a little more olive oil. Season with salt and pepper, then cover with foil.

Roast in the oven for 40-45 minutes or until outside starts to crisp.

CAULIFLOWER SALAD

INGREDIENTS

2 tablespoons olive oil
1 1/2 teaspoons cumin
1 1/2 teaspoons paprika
1 teaspoon salt
1/2 teaspoon black pepper
1 head cauliflower, cut into florets
1 can chickpeas, drained
12 cherry tomatoes, cut in half
4 ounces arugula, shredded
1/4 cup feta, crumbled
Juice of half a lemon

Parve/Vegan option: omit cheese

Egg Free   Gluten Free   Nut Free

Parve Option   Vegan Option   Serves: 6~8

INSTRUCTIONS

Preheat oven to 400°F. Line a cookie sheet with parchment paper.

In a large bowl, mix the olive oil, cumin, paprika, salt and pepper. Toss the cauliflower and chickpeas in the mixture to coat. Spread the cauliflower and chickpeas in a single layer on the baking sheet.

Roast for 20 minutes, until cauliflower browns slightly. Transfer cauliflower to a bowl. Let stand for 5 minutes to cool. Add in tomatoes, arugula and feta and toss everything together. Squeeze lemon juice on top.

DESSERTS

TRIPLE BERRY TART

INGREDIENTS

For the crust:
1/4 cup sugar
1/4 teaspoon salt
1 teaspoon vanilla
1 teaspoon orange zest
2 cups flaked coconut
1/3 cup coconut oil

For the filling:
2 cups berries
1 tablespoon honey or agave
1 tablespoon jam or preserves
Zest and juice of half a lemon
1 teaspoon vanilla
1 tablespoon of almond meal

INSTRUCTIONS

Preheat oven to 325°F.

Combine sugar, vanilla, zest, and coconut in a bowl. Add coconut oil and mix until coconut mixture is coated. Press into 9" tart pan.

Bake for 10-15 minutes or until crust is golden.

In a medium bowl, add all the berries, honey, jam, zest, lemon juice., and vanilla. Stir until mixed. Stir in the almond meal to thicken it all up a bit. Pour into the cooled crust.

Bake for 20-25 minutes.

Egg Free

Gluten Free

Parve

Vegan Option

Serves: 8

SPICED UP CARROT CAKE

INGREDIENTS

1/2 pound baby carrots (1 1/2 cups)
1 cup plus 2 tablespoons orange juice
9 eggs separated
3/4 teaspoon salt
1 1/2 cup sugar
1 tablespoon vanilla extract
3/4 cup matza meal
3/4 cup matza cake meal
1 1/4 cup ground walnuts
1 teaspoon cinnamon
1/4 teaspoon ground fresh ginger
1/4 teaspoon allspice
zest of 1 lemon

INSTRUCTIONS

Preheat oven to 350°F.

Cover peeled carrots with 1 cup of water and 1 cup of orange juice in a saucepan. Cook over medium heat until carrots are fork tender, about 30 minutes.

Puree the carrots using a fork (or hand blender) and set aside.

Beat egg whites with salt until foamy. Slowly add 1/2 cup of the sugar and beat until there are glossy stiff peaks. Set aside.

In the mixer, beat the egg yolks until very pale. Add the remaining cup of sugar

Parve

Serves: 8-10

and beat until very thick.

Blend the dry ingredients together in a bowl. Add dry ingredients, vanilla extract, orange juice, and lemon zest to the eggs. Mix until just blended. Add carrot puree and mix just until combined.

Gently fold in the egg whites until just blended.

Spray/oil/butter the bottom of a cake pan. Pour in the cake batter. Bake cake until it springs back when gently pressed in the middle, 40 minutes.

GLUTEN FREE CHOCOLATE CAKE

INGREDIENTS

3 ounces chocolate ,chopped
(or use chocolate chips)
3/4 cup (1 1/2 sticks) butter, cubed
large eggs, separated
2 tablespoons sugar
teaspoons vanilla extract

For parve meals:
Use 3/4 cup coconut oil instead
of butter

INSTRUCTIONS

Preheat oven to 350°F.

Butter a 9-inch spring form pan. Line bottom of pan with parchment paper or waxed paper; butter/oil paper. Wrap outside of pan with foil.

Stir chocolate and butter in heavy medium saucepan over low heat until melted and smooth. Remove from heat. Cool to lukewarm, stirring often.

Using electric mixer, beat egg yolks and tablespoons sugar in a large bowl until mixture is very thick and pale, about 3 minutes. Fold lukewarm chocolate mixture into yolk mixture, then fold in vanilla extract.

Gluten Free   Nut Free   Parve Option   Serves: 8-10

Using clean dry beaters, whip egg whites in another large bowl until soft peaks form.

Gradually add remaining 6 tablespoons sugar, beating until medium-firm peaks form.

Fold whites into chocolate mixture in three additions.

Pour batter into prepared pan and bake cake until top is puffed and cracked and tester inserted into center comes out with some moist crumbs attached, about 50 minutes.

Cool cake in pan on rack (cake will fall).

Gently press down crusty top to make evenly thick cake. Using a knife, cut around pan sides to loosen cake. Remove pan sides. Place serving plate or cardboard round atop cake. Invert cake and peel off parchment paper.

Serve as it or top it with a glaze. I think a dollop of whipped cream is divine with this chocolate goodness.

NUTELLA TARTLET

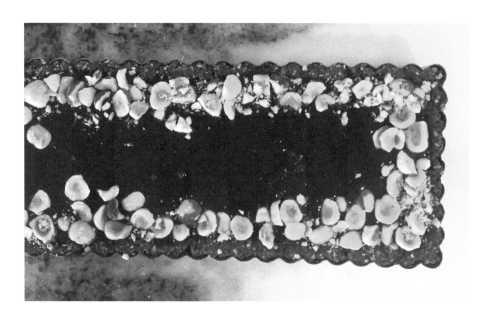

INGREDIENTS

For the crust:
2 cups nuts
1 pinch kosher salt
1 tablespoon sugar
6 tablespoons coconut oil

For the filling:
16 ounces chocoloate
1 15 ounce can coconut milk
1/2 teaspoon vanilla
1 cup toasted hazelnuts, choppe

Egg Free

Gluten Free

Parve

Vegan Option

Serves: 8-10

INSTRUCTIONS

Preheat oven to 350°F. Grease a pie or tart pan.

Put nuts, sugar, and salt in a food processor and pulse until ground. Pulse in the melted butter.

Press the mixture evenly into the prepared pie pan. Make sure you even it out.

Bake 12 to 15 minutes, or until browned and fairly set. It may be a little soft when it comes out of the oven; don't worry, it will firm up.

Place the coarsely chopped chocolate in a medium-sized bowl. Set aside.

In a small saucepan over medium-hig flame, heat the coconut milk until bubble just begin to appear around the edges.

Pour the coconut milk over the choppe chocolate and let stand without stirring fo 5 minutes. Stir the mixture until glossy ar smooth.

Add the vanilla extract and stir un incorporated.

Pour ganache into the crust. Scatter th hazelnuts on top.

Refrigerate until firm, about an hour.

BANANA CLOUD

INGREDIENTS

- eggs, separated
- cup sugar
- /4 teaspoon salt
- teaspoon vanilla
- ripe bananas, mashed
- /4 cup potato starch

Gluten Free

Nut Free

Parve

Serves: 8~10

INSTRUCTIONS

Preheat oven to 350°F. Grease two bread pans.

Beat egg yolks until thickened. Add the sugar, salt and vanilla and beat until light. Stir in the bananas and potato starch until combined.

In a separate bowl, beat the egg whites until stiff peaks form. Gently fold the whites into the egg yolk mixture.

Pour the batter into the prepared pans and bake for 30 minutes or until a skewer inserted into the center comes out clean.

CHERRY CLAFOUTIS

INGREDIENTS

1 lb 10oz pitted cherries (fresh or frozen)
3 tbsp kirsch, grappa or any nice liqueur
6 tbsp sugar
4 large eggs
1 vanilla bean (or 2 tsp of vanilla extract)
2/3 cup matza cake meal
1 1/4 cups milk (for the non-dairy option, use Almond, Coconut or Soy Milk)
Pinch of salt

Nut Free

Parve Option

Serves: 8-10

INSTRUCTIONS

Preheat oven to 400°F and butter a 9" pie dish.

Toss the cherries with kirsch and 2 tablespoons of the sugar in a bowl and let stand for 30 minutes.

Strain the liquid from the cherries (DON'T DISCARD!).

Whisk the eggs, drained cherry liquid, seeds from the vanilla bean (or vanilla extract), and the remaining 4 tbsp of sugar in a bowl until combined. Gradually whisk in the cake meal, then add the milk and salt. Whisk until smooth.

Spread the cherries in the dish and pour the batter on top. You can fill the dish until just near the top.

Bake for 35-45 minutes, until the top is brown and the center is firm. Serve this warm or at room temperature.

LEMON CAKE

Parve

Serves: 8-10

INGREDIENTS

2 lemons
12 tbsp unsalted butter or coconut oil
1 1/4 cups sugar
2 large eggs, plus an egg yolk
1 1/3 cups almond meal
1/2 cup matza cake meal
2 tsp baking powder
1 1/3 cups plain coconut yogurt

Top this lovely cake with freshly whipped cream!

INSTRUCTIONS

Preheat the oven to 325°F. Butter an 8 inch cake or spring form pan, and line the bottom with parchment paper.

Grate the zest. Squeeze the juice from the lemons (you'll get about 6 tbsp of juice).

Cream together the butter, 3/4 cups of the sugar and the zest in a large bowl until light and fluffy. Beat in the eggs one at a time.

In a separate bowl, whisk the flours and baking powder together. Stir into the butter mixture. Add the yogurt and 3 tablespoons of the lemon juice. Spread the batter in the pan and bake for 30-40 minutes, or until the center springs back when pressed.

Stir the remaining 1/2 cup of sugar and remaining lemon juice in a saucepan over low hear until all the sugar has dissolved. Let it cool.

Transfer cake to a wire rack and drizzle with syrup. Cool for 30 minutes. Invert the cake onto a plate, remove pan and peel off the paper. Cool completely.

CHOCOLATE
CRACKLE COOKIES

Gluten Free

Parve

Yield: 20

INGREDIENTS

5 cups confectioner's sugar
1 cup Dutch pressed cocoa powder
2 tsp cinnamon
1 tsp cardamom
1 tbsp espresso powder
1/2 teaspoon sea salt (for batter)
6 large egg whites, room temperature
1 tbsp pure vanilla extract
10 ounces semi-sweet chocolate
2 ounces bittersweet chocolate
1/2 cup hazelnut meal
2 teaspoon sea salt (for topping)

INSTRUCTIONS

Preheat oven to 350°F. Grease a parchmen
lined baking sheet.

In a medium bowl, sift together confectioner
sugar, cocoa powder, cinnamon, cardamom, se
salt, and espresso powder. Combine thorough
with a fork.

Add egg whites and vanilla and whisk un
dough forms. Add semi-sweet and bitterswe
chocolate. Stir in hazelnut meal. Refrigerate f
10 minutes.

Using a melon baller, form mounds on yo
baking sheet. The cookies will spread out in th
oven, so don't press them down. Sprinkle with
little bit of sea salt.

Bake for 15 minutes, until the tops crackle. L
cool at least 10 minutes before serving.

MATZA CRACK
AKA CHOCOLATE ALMOND BRITTLE

INGREDIENTS

2 cups coarsely crumbled matzas
1 1/2 cups sliced almonds
1/2 cup (1 stick) butter or coconut oil
1/2 cup packed light-brown sugar
1/2 teaspoon salt
2 cups semisweet chocolate chips

Egg Free	Parve	Vegan Option	Serves: 8

INSTRUCTIONS

Preheat oven to 325°F. Line a large rimmed baking sheet with parchment.

In a bowl, toss matzo pieces with almonds.

In a saucepan, bring butter or coconut oil, sugar, salt, and 2 tablespoons water to a boil over medium, stirring constantly. Working quickly, drizzle matzo mixture with syrup, and toss. Spread mixture onto prepared sheet. Bake until golden, about 30 minutes.

Remove from oven; sprinkle with chocolate chips. Let chocolate melt for 5 minutes then use a knife to spread chocolate over matza brittle.

Refrigerate until chocolate has set. Break into pieces and serve.

I remember the first time my cousin Erika made these for Passover. I got addicted right then and there. Passover isn't complete without these in my belly.

PECAN COOKIES

Gluten Free

Parve

Yield: 24

INGREDIENTS

6 oz pecans (1 1/2 cups)
1 cup sugar
1/4 cup potato starch
1/4 teaspoon salt
1/4 teaspoon cinnamon
3 large egg whites, lightly beaten

INSTRUCTIONS

Preheat oven to 375°F. Line a large baking she
with parchment paper.

Coarsely chop 1 cup of the pecans and set asid

Pulse remaining 1/2 cup pecans in a foo
processor with sugar, potato starch, salt, ar
cinnamon until finely ground (be careful not
pulse to a paste), then stir into the egg white
Mix in the cup of chopped pecans.

Drop 1/2 tablespoons of batter 2 inches apart
baking sheet and bake until cookies are light
browned and slightly puffed, 15 to 17 minute
Slide parchment onto a rack and cool cookie
completely (cookies will crisp as they cool), the
remove from paper.

N'ICE CREAM

INGREDIENTS

bananas, peeled

For tropical ice cream:
/4 cup frozen mango
/4 cup frozen pineapple
tablespoons coconut oil
/2 teaspoon vanilla

For blueberry ice cream:
/2 cup frozen blueberries
tablespoons coconut oil
/2 teaspoon vanilla

For green tea ice cream:
1/2 teaspoons Green Tea Powder
1/2 tablespoons Honey, more to taste

INSTRUCTIONS

Peel the bananas and slice them thickly. Freeze until solid, around 2 hours.

Put them in the blender or food processor and turn the machine on to blend them.

Once the mixture is smooth, blend in the ingredients for the flavored ice cream.

Transfer to a freezer container and freeze until solid.

DISHES FOR THE PASSOVER WEEK

POPOVERS

INGREDIENTS

1 1/2 cups water
1/2 cup sunflower oil
1/2 teaspoon salt
1 tablespoon sugar
1/2 cup matza cake meal
1 cup matza meal
6 eggs

Nut Free

Parve

Yield: 6-12

INSTRUCTIONS

Preheat oven to 400°F. Grease a standard muffin tin or a 6-cup popover pan

Put the water, oil, salt, and sugar in a saucepan, and bring to a boil.

Remove the mixture from the heat. Stir in the cake meal, then the matza meal; the dough will be very stiff. Transfer it to bowl of a mixer and let it cool to lukewarm.

Crack the eggs into a large measuring cup. With your mixer running, gradually pour the unbeaten eggs into the lukewarm batter. Beat till smooth; scrape the sides and bottom of the bowl, and beat till smooth again.

Scoop the stiff batter into the prepared pa filling the cups about 3/4 full.

Place the pan in the center of the ove and bake for 10 minutes. Reduce the ove heat to 325°F, and bake for an addition 30 minutes. Popovers should be a mediu golden brown.

To check if they're done, pull one out of th pan and break it open; the interior shou be mildly moist, but not soggy. Remove th popovers from the oven, and place them c a rack to cool.

FRENCH TOAST MATZA BREI

Nut Free

Parve Option

Yield: 2

INGREDIENTS

- eggs
- tablespoons milk
- 1/2 teaspoon vanilla extract
- 1/2 teaspoon brown sugar
- matzas
- tablespoons butter or coconut oil

INSTRUCTIONS

In a bowl, crack the eggs and whisk together with the milk, vanilla and brown sugar.

Break the matza into tiny pieces and add into the egg mixture. Mix thoroughly to make sure the matzas soak in the moisture.

In a pan over moderate heat, melt a tablespoon of butter. When foamy, pour in half the brei batter. Fry until browned on both sides, about 1-2 minutes per side.

MATZA BREI
TOPPED WITH FRIED EGGS

Nut Free

Parve Option

Yield: 2

INGREDIENTS

For the matza brei:
2 eggs
2 tablespoons milk
1/2 teaspoon salt
1/4 teaspoon black pepper
3 matzas
2 tablespoons butter or oil

For the eggs:
2 eggs
1 tablespoon butter or oil
1 tablespoon za'atar
3 cherry tomatoes, halved
1 teaspoon parsley, chopped

INSTRUCTIONS

In a bowl, crack the eggs and whisk together with the milk, salt and pepper.

Break the matza into tiny pieces and add into the egg mixture. Mix thoroughly to make sure the matza soak in the moisture.

In a pan over moderate heat, melt a tablespoon of butter. When foamy, pour in half the brei batter. Fry until browned on both sides, about 1-2 minutes per side. Transfer to plate and cook the other brei.

Make eggs: Fry the eggs in the butter (or oil). Place on top of brei, sprinkle with za'atar, tomatoes and parsley

GREEN SHAKSHUKA

INGREDIENTS

tablespoons olive oil
tablespoons schug
large onion, sliced
cloves garlic, crushed
teaspoon ground cumin
cups greens (spinach and kale)
eggs
tablespoons yogurt
/4 cup crumbled feta
ea salt
lack pepper

Gluten Free

Nut Free

Parve Option

Serves: 4

INSTRUCTIONS

Heat oven to 400°F.

On the stove top, warm the olive oil in an oven-roof pan over medium heat.

Add the schug, onion, garlic, cumin and two ig pinches of salt. Cook until the onions are oftened. Add the greens and simmer over medium heat until they wilt. Salt and pepper to aste.

Depending on the number of eggs you are sing, make a little divot in the sauce for each. Gently break an egg into each hole, making ure not to break the yolks. Spoon yogurt in etween the eggs.
prinkle the whole pan with feta.

lace the pan in the oven and cook until the gg whites are set but the yolks are still runny.

PEPPER SHAKSHUKA

INGREDIENTS

2 tablespoons olive oil
2 tablespoons schug
1 tablespoon tomato paste
2 red peppers, cut into chunks
1 yellow pepper, cut into chunks
4 cloves garlic, crushed
1 teaspoon ground cumin
4 cups of diced tomatoes
4 eggs
Salt and black pepper

INSTRUCTIONS

Heat oven to 400°F.

On the stove top, warm the olive oil in a oven-proof pan over medium heat. Ad the schug, tomato paste, peppers, garl cumin and two big pinches of salt. Coo until the peppers have softened.

Add the diced tomatoes and simm over medium heat until the sau thickens. Salt and pepper to taste.

Make four little divots in the sauce. Gen break an egg into each hole, making su not to break the yolks.

Place the pan in the oven and cook un the egg whites are set but the yolks a still runny.

Shakshuka is amazingly versatile. You can use almost any vegetable in the base! Try it with leeks, Swiss chard or jalapeños. Use leftover tomato sauce. Have fun with it.

LOX & ASPARAGUS FRITTATA

INGREDIENTS

tablespoons olive oil, divided
eggs
/4 cup sour cream or yogurt
small onion, chopped
/2 lb asparagus, trimmed
2 ounces lox, cut into 1" pieces
/2 teaspoon salt
/8 teaspoon black pepper
tablespoons parsley, chopped

Nut Free   Parve   Yield: 6-12

INSTRUCTIONS

reheat oven to 350°F.

Cut asparagus into 3/4" pieces.

n a bowl, combine eggs, sour cream, salt, pepper and parsley.

n a cast iron skillet over a medium high ame, heat a tablespoon of olive oil. Cook nion, stirring occasionally, until softened, -4 minutes.

Add the asparagus and cook another 3 minutes.

Add a tablespoon of oil to the pan and our in the egg mixture.

Reduce heat to law. Cook, without stirring, until edges set, about 5 minutes. Transfer pan to oven and bake until golden brown, 25-30 minutes.

MISO GINGER GREEN SALAD

Meat

Meat

Meat

Meat

INGREDIENTS

1/4 head green cabbage
1 cup snow peas
1 bunch broccoli
1 bunch broccoli leaves
4 scallions
1/4 cup dill, chopped
1/4 cup mint, chopped
1 large carrot
1/4 cup miso paste
Zest and juice of half a lemon
1 tablespoon grated ginger
2 tablespoons rice vinegar
1 tablespoon toasted sesame oil
1/4 cup cilantro, chopped

INSTRUCTIONS

Chop all the greens and place in a bow
Grate the carrots into the greens.

Mix the dressing ingredients un
combined. If the dressing is too thick, ac
water a few drops at a time until desire
consistency is reached. Drizzle on top c
the salad.

Toss salad to coat.

HOOMOOS STUFFED SWEET POTATO

Parve Option

Serves: 8

INGREDIENTS

Per sweet potato:
1 sweet potato
1 tablespoon olive oil
4 cremini mushrooms, sliced
1/2 teaspoon garlic powder
2 tablespoons hoomoos (hummus)
4 cherry tomatoes quartered
1 tablespoon parsley, chopped

Optional: add a fried egg on top

INSTRUCTIONS

Preheat the oven to 400°F. Line a baking sheet with foil.

Pierce each sweet potato several times with the tines of a fork and brush with olive oil. Place the sweet potatoes on the baking sheet and bake until tender, about 45 minutes. Make a slit in the top of each sweet potato.

In the meantime, heat oil in a skillet over a medium high flame. Cook the cremini mushrooms until softened, 4-5 minutes. Season with garlic powder, salt and pepper.

Assembly: mash the inside of the sweet potato a bit within the peel. Spread the hoomoos, then top with mushrooms, tomatoes and parsley. Lay a fried egg on top for extra protein.

FLOURLESS GNOCCHI

INGREDIENTS

6 Yukon gold potatoes
1 1/2 cups potato starch
1 1/2 cups almond flour
1 teaspoon salt
2 eggs

 Gluten Free Nut Free Parve Serves: 8-10

INSTRUCTIONS

Put unpeeled potatoes in a large pot and fill with enough cold water to cover the potatoes by at least 2 inches. Bring to a boil over medium-high heat. Reduce the heat to medium and simmer the potatoes until they are fork tender, 30 to 35 minutes. Drain the potatoes and set them aside to cool.

In a bowl, whisk together the potato starch, almond meal, and salt.

Once you can handle them, peel the potatoes. Cut them in half and pass them through a ricer (or use a potato masher to puree them) into a bowl. Add the eggs and blend well. Then, add the starch mixture and mix with your hands until a dough forms that holds together but is not too sticky. Cover the dough with a towel and let it rest for 30 minutes.

Fill a pot with salted water and bring to a boil.

On a clean surface, sprinkle potato starch. Grab a handful of dough and roll it into a rope, about 3/4 inch thick. Using a sharp knife, cut every 3/4 inch. Use a fork to make impressions on each piece.

Cook gnocchi in batches by dropping them in the water. When they are done, they will pop up to the surface.

Serve with your favorite pasta sauce.

SWEET CREPES

Gluten Free

Nut Free

Parve Option

Yield: 12

INGREDIENTS

6 eggs
6 tablespoons potato starch
1/2 cup water or milk
1/2 teaspoon salt
1/2 teaspoon vanilla extract
1 tablespoon sugar

INSTRUCTIONS

Place all the ingredients in a bowl and whisk until smooth.

Let the batter sit for at least 15 minutes (or leave it in the refrigerator overnight).

Heat a small skillet or crepe pan over a moderate flame. Put a bit of butter or oil to grease the pan.

Pour 1/3 cup of batter into the pan and swirl to coat the bottom evenly. Cook for 1-2 minutes or until the sides begin to brown and bubbles pop in the batter.

Flip over and cook for another minute or until crepe is golden brown. Transfer to a plate and fold into quarters. Repeat with remaining crepes.

Serve immediately with your choice of toppings (pictured here is sweet ricotta, berries and honey).

MATCHA CREPE CAKE

INGREDIENTS

For the crepes:
Double the recipe for Sweet Crepes

For the Pastry Cream:
1 egg
2 tablespoons tapioca starch
2 tablespoons granulated sugar
1 cup milk
1 teaspoon vanilla extract
1 teaspoon hot water
2 tablespoons heavy cream, whipped

For the Matcha Whipped Cream:
2 cups heavy cream
2 tablespoons matcha
1 tablespoon sugar

This is a showstopper.
Crepe cake is my all-time favorite dessert and I can't imagine a special occasion without one. The matcha (green tea powder) adds a unique flavor but if you want a plain ol' crepe cake, omit the matcha from the cream.

INSTRUCTIONS

Make the pastry cream (best done the night before so it thickens): In a small bowl, add egg, starch and sugar and beat until smooth.

In a saucepan over low heat, being milk almost to a simmer. Remove from heat and slowly whisk the milk into the egg mixture. Return the combine mixture to the saucepan and cook while stirring for 5 minutes, until thickened and just comes to a boil.

Remove mixture from heat. Add vanilla and hot water. Stir until smooth. Set aside to cool until firm.

When the pastry cream has cooled, fold in the 2 tablespoons of whipped heavy cream. Refrigerate until thick (best overnight). Make 24 crepes using the previous recipe.

In a mixer, whip the heavy cream with matcha and sugar until peaks form. Gently fold the whipped cream into the pastry cream.

Place one crepe on a large cake plate. With an offset spatula, completely cover the crepe with a thin layer of the pastry cream mixture. Cover with another crepe and repeat until you finish all the layers. Top the cake with another thin layer of cream and dust with matcha to complete the look.

Refrigerate cake for at least 2 hours.

Gluten
Free

Nut Free

Serves:
8-10

ACKNOWLEDGMENTS

I am so grateful to the many people who helped bring this book to life.

First of all, I am indebted to my wonderful peeps who immediately accepted the challenge to te my recipes and gave me incredible feedback that helped shape this book. Molly Przetycki Fiedle Alison Urkowitz Green; Tracy Kaplan; Anya, Bella and Zack Levison; Alyssa Monks; and Christir O'Donnell: your comments really helped me edit the final recipes (and chuck some of the one that simply didn't make the grade).

Kati Frisch Grossman - thanks for your friendship, love, support and the edits.

To my dear friend, Lori Landau: your help and support have given me wings. Thank you for yo patience, friendship, love, caring, editing, brainstorming, styling...EVERYTHING! I am incredib lucky and grateful. You inspire me to do more and be more.

To Oliver Krisch, who taught me to properly light, stage and photograph my food. If only I ha known these tricks sooner!!! Thank you for taking so much time, care and effort to help me. Mo important, thank you for being so open to my silliness and crazy ideas and for bringing them all life. Your photos are beautiful and your work is meticulous. To Morgen: thank you for babysittir and tasting some of the recipes.

To Meredith McBride Kipp: your creativity and craft are so incredible that not even the fog of infant and toddler can shake you. Your love, support and friendship make me so very happy. I st think, "Gosh, we could have been friends for 25 years already if only we'd listened to our moms.

To my amazing supporters - my parents and in-laws are incredible. You make me feel like I can anything I set my sights on and give me the support in order to actualize my dreams. Thank yo for everything.

And to my core: Zack, Bella and Anya. You are my heart. I am so proud of the family we hav created and love spending countless hours talking about, cooking and savoring food with you - the kitchen and beyond.